We Can Chat!

by Carmel Reilly

illustrated by Ana Sebastián

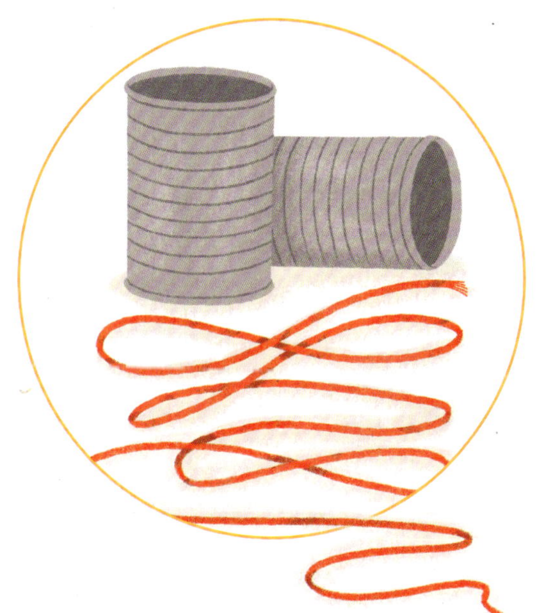

OXFORD
UNIVERSITY PRESS

Jazz huffs and gets up.

Zak puffs and gets up.

Zak yells to Jazz.

Yes, we can chat on the bus!

Quick, pack the bag!

Jazz and Zak chat
on and on.

Jazz and Zak yak
till sunset.

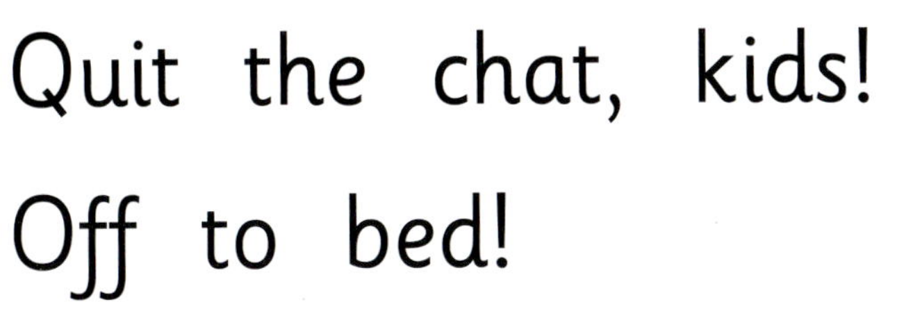
Quit the chat, kids!
Off to bed!

Got a can?
I will check.

Zak is quick.

Chop off the zigzag bits.

It will be
fun to chat!
buzz buzz

It will be fun
to chat in bed!

I cannot chat.

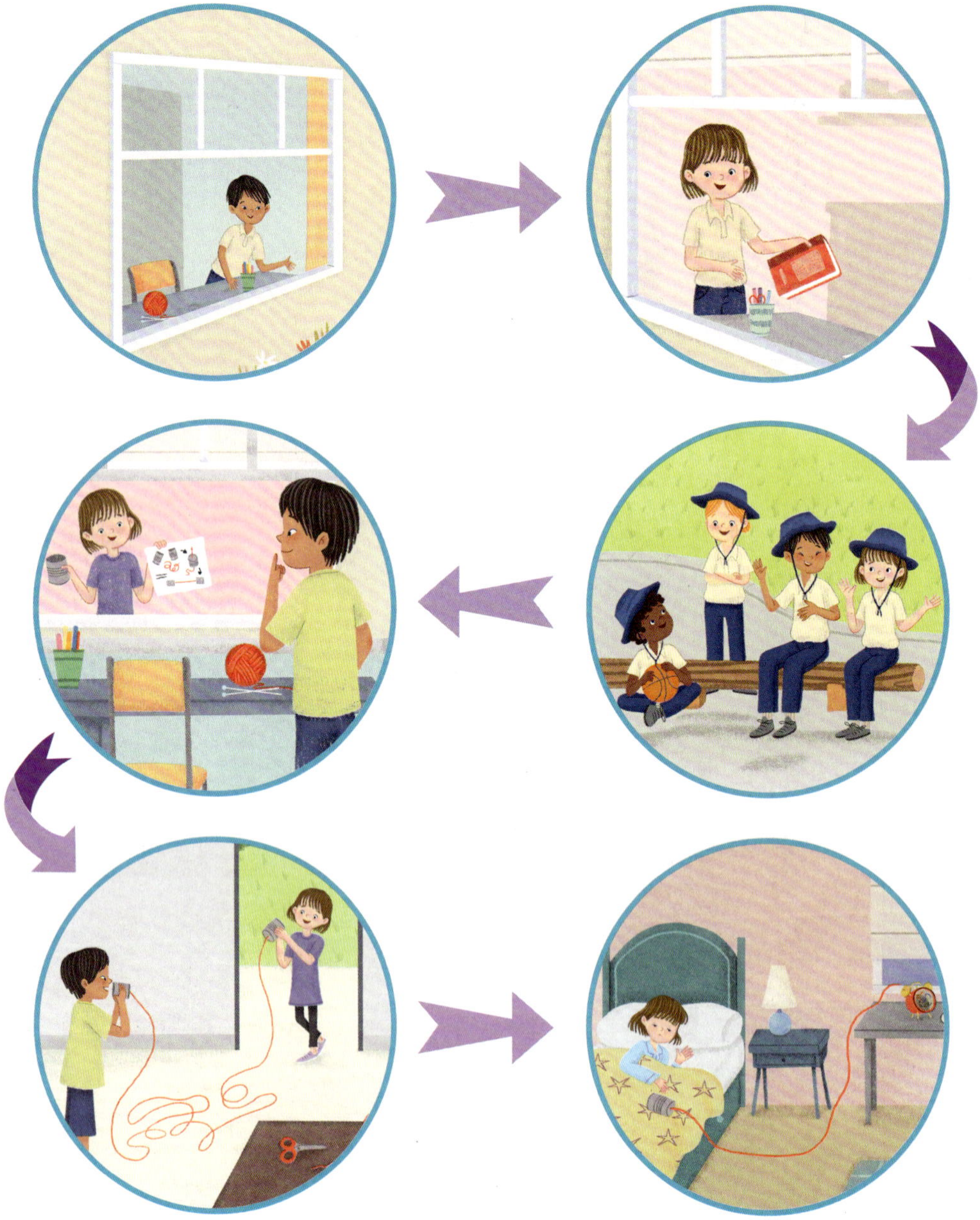

Encourage students to use the pictures to retell the story.